Focus on Ghana

Heather C. Hudak

A Crabtree Forest Book

Crabtree Publishing
crabtreebooks.com

Author: Heather C. Hudak

Series research and development: Janine Deschenes

Editorial director: Kathy Middleton

Editor: Crystal Sikkens

Proofreader: Melissa Boyce

Design: Tammy McGarr

Print and production coordinator: Katherine Berti

IMAGE CREDITS

Dreamstime: Lisamildes, p 37 (bottom);

Shutterstock: Dietmar Temps, cover (top left), p 32; Anton Ivanov, title page, p 5, p 26 (top), p 35 (top), p 40; Charles William Adofo, p 11 (top); Gerhard Pettersson, p 14 (bottom); Margus Vilbas Photography, p 14 (top); Nataly Reinch, p 20 (bottom), p 28 (top), p 29 (top), p 33 (bottom); Fela Sanu, p 21 (top); Truba7113, p 24 (bottom), p 25 (top); nicolasdecorte, p 27; Richard Juilliart, p 28 (bottom); Nancy Haggarty, p 29 (bottom); Terence Toh Chin Eng, p 31 (bottom inset); Delali Adogla-Bessa, p 31 (bottom); K.Kyere p 35 (bottom); john afunya, p 37 (top); schusterbauer.com, p 43 (top); Delali Adogla-Bessa, p 43 (bottom); wlablack, p 45 (top); TG23, p 45 (middle);

iStock: sanjeri, p 4; fratdj, p 21 (right middle);

Wikimedia Commons: Charles J. Sharp, p 13 (bottom right); Rtevels, p 15 (middle); Richard New Forest, p 17 (left inset); Great Britain. Parliament. House of Commons, p 21 (bottom); Public Domain, p 22 (bottom); J Nash, p 22 (top); Fquasie, p 28 (middle); NanaYawBotar, p 30 (inset); Benson Ibeabuchi, p 34; Macabe5387, p 39 (bottom); The Childrens Museum of Indianapolis, p 39 (top); SAgbley, p 41 (top);

Ghana-2020 © The Hunger Project, p 44 (top)

UNDPL, p 44 (bottom)

Crabtree Publishing

crabtreebooks.com 800-387-7650

In Canada: We acknowledge the financial support of the Government of Canada through the Canada Book Fund for our publishing activities.

Hardcover 978-1-0398-0643-6
Paperback 978-1-0398-0669-6
Ebook (pdf) 978-1-0398-0695-5
Epub 978-1-0398-0722-8

Published in Canada
Crabtree Publishing
616 Welland Avenue
St. Catharines, Ontario
L2M 5V6

Published in the United States
Crabtree Publishing
347 Fifth Avenue
Suite 1402-145
New York, New York, 10016

Library and Archives Canada Cataloguing in Publication
Available at Library and Archives Canada

Library of Congress Cataloging-in-Publication Data
Available at the Library of Congress

Printed in the U.S.A./012023/CG20220815

Contents

Introduction

There are many **smallholder farms** that produce groundnuts, which are a very important protein for both humans and animals.

Snapshot of a Farming Village

Early mornings are a busy time in the rural farming village of Savelugu, Ghana. Both men and women rise early to prepare for the long day ahead. Breakfast is the most important meal of the day. It often includes a bowl of *koko*, which is a spicy corn porridge, and *koso*, which are fried bean fritters. After breakfast, local men ride their bikes to the fields where they work. They prepare the land for **cultivation** and growth.

The women rise before the rest of the family each morning. They start the household chores and prepare the food for the day. Then, they join their husbands on the farm and help them work the land. Some men have more than one wife, and they take turns doing the housework. Older children also help out around the house before and after school.

After harvesting fruit, a woman peels and prepares it for a meal with her family.

Family Hierarchy

Women do as much as 70 percent of the work on the farms. They plant seeds, weed the land, harvest crops, and process the final product. They also sell their products in their community, which earns them a small income of their own. Some even run their own farms. Women do not have the same rights to their family's land or property as men, however. They also have very little education compared to the men in Savelugu. The male head of the household has total control of the family's wealth. He makes all decisions, and his word is final. Everyone else must do as he says, including his wife.

The oldest male child inherits the family's **assets** when the father dies. He must then care for his mother and any siblings that still live at home. Girls are expected to marry into another family. If their husband dies, they remarry as soon as possible. In most cases, they have very little wealth and power of their own.

Small but Mighty

Ghana is a small country in western Africa, but it is one of great importance. It was the first Black **sub-Saharan** African nation to gain independence from **colonial** rule. It is rich in **natural resources**, making it one of the wealthiest countries on the African continent. Under British rule, it was known as the Gold Coast. Today, its official name is the **Republic** of Ghana. It paved the way for other nations to break free of colonial rule.

Rich Culture

The country has a population of about 32 million, and most people are Ghanaian by birth. They belong to one large ethnic group with at least 75 subgroups. Akan is the largest subgroup, making up about 47 percent of the population. Christianity is the dominant religion, and English is the official language. Many Ghanaians speak other languages as well. About 16 percent of people speak Asante, while about 12 percent speak Fante.

Diverse Geography

Ghana sits at the center of the world. It is located close to both the equator and the **Greenwich meridian**. It is situated along the Gulf of Guinea to the south. Togo sits to the east of Ghana, and Côte d'Ivoire lies to the west. Burkina Faso makes up the northern border.

Ghana is the 82nd largest country on Earth. It is slightly smaller than the U.S. state of Oregon. The country spans 92,098 square miles (238,533 sq. km), which includes 87,854 square miles (227,540 sq. km) of land and 4,244 square miles (10,992 sq. km) of water. Ghana's diverse geography includes everything from beaches and savannas to forests and coastlines. Accra is the capital of Ghana. Other major cities include Kumasi, Tamale, Cape Coast, and Sekondi-Takoradi.

Accra has a population of just over 4 million people.

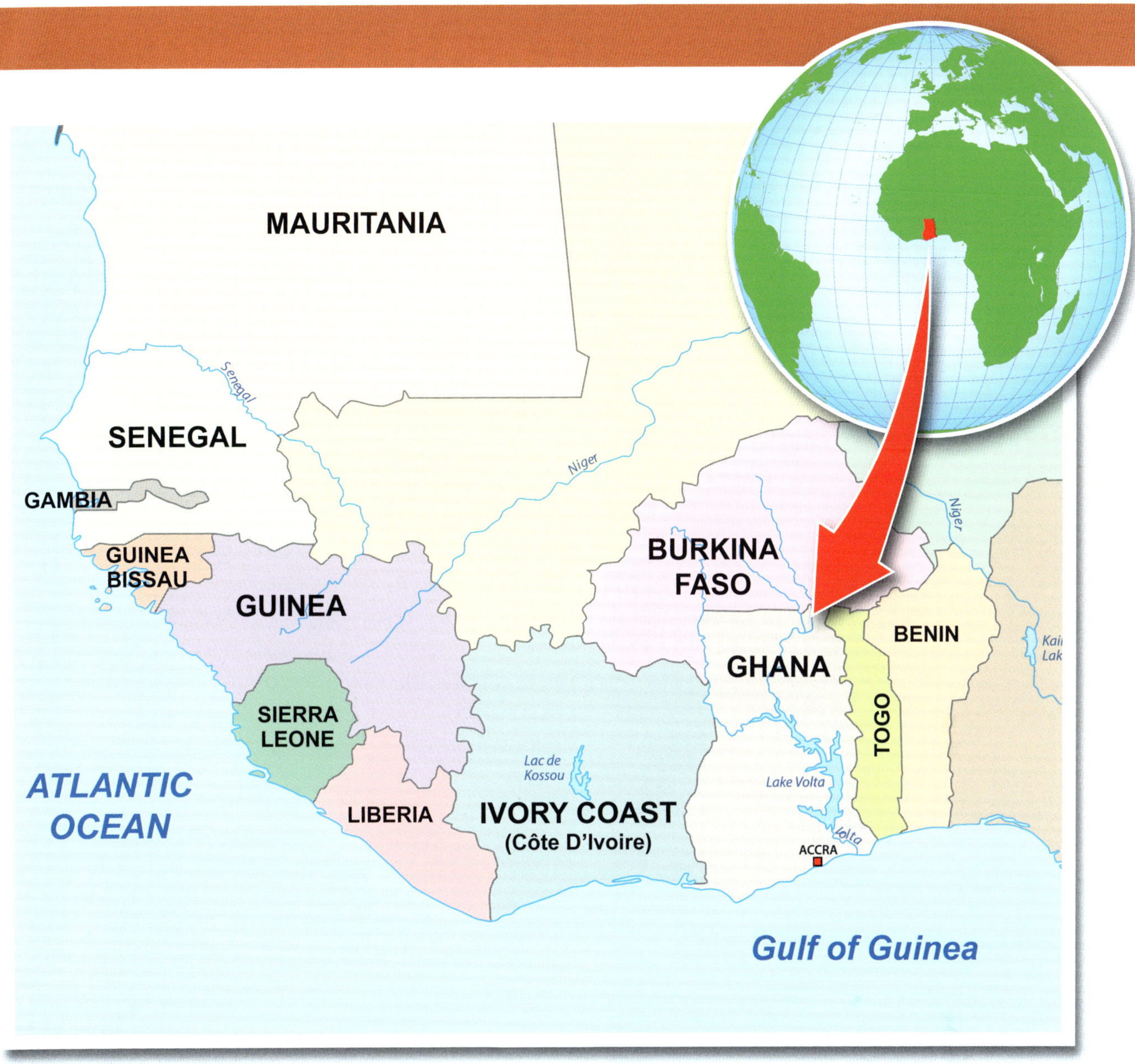

AT A GLANCE

- **OFFICIAL NAME:** Republic of Ghana
- **NATIONAL CAPITAL:** Accra
- **POPULATION:** 32,346,363
- **OFFICIAL LANGUAGES:** English
- **LAND AREA:** 87,854 square miles (227,540 sq. km)

CHAPTER 1

Fertile Lands

coastal region

forest region

northern savanna region

Most of Ghana is made up of low-lying plains. About half of the country is no more than 500 feet (152 m) above sea level. Severely eroded plateaus cover the south-central part of the country, creating hills, valleys, and flat uplands.

Geographic Regions

Ghana is divided into three key geographic regions. The smallest is the coastal region. It is a thriving **economic** area known for its fishing industry. Tall grasses and scrub cover the land, along with giant anthills and baobab trees. Most people in this region work as fishers or small-scale farmers. Despite its small size, there are more large cities in the coastal region than the other two regions. Accra, Cape Coast, and Sekondi-Takoradi are all found in the coastal region.

The forest region accounts for about one-third of Ghana's land. It has a wealth of natural resources, such as **cacao**, minerals, and timber. Kumasi is the largest city in this region, and there are few other urban areas. The western part of this region is known for its thick tropical rain forests. Many have been cut down to allow for farmlands and human settlements. In the east, this region consists mainly of grasslands and savanna forests. **Deciduous** forests comprise the northern part of the forest region.

The northern savanna is the largest region. It covers about two-thirds of the country, but it has the fewest people living in it. This region has very little precipitation, so the environment is dry and harsh. Only a few grasses and low trees grow in this area. It is not well developed, and most of the farming done in this region is for **subsistence** only. Irrigation systems are used to bring water to farmlands.

BURKINA FASO
BENIN
CÔTE D'IVOIRE
TOGO
GHANA
Upper East
Bolgatanga
Upper West
Wa
Sisili
Kulpawn
Black Volta
White Volta
Oti
Tamale
Northern
Daka
Black Volta
Oti
Brong-Ahafo
Tain
Pru
Sunyani
Lake Volta
Ashanti
Afram
Tano
Kumasi
Anum
Ho
Eastern
Volta
Birim
Koforidua
Ofin
Tano
Ankobra
Greater Accra
Western
Central
ACCRA
Pra
Cape Coast
Sekondi-Takoradi
Cape Three Points
Gulf of Guinea

The Adomi Bridge, which spans the Volta River, is Ghana's longest suspension bridge.

Most fishing on Lake Bosumtwi is done using nets that are thrown into the water to trap fish.

Water World

There are many lagoons, rivers, streams, and sandy beaches along Ghana's 335-mile-long (539 km) coastline. Many are navigable only by canoe. Part of the country is located in the Volta River basin. This mighty river is 1,000 miles (1,600 km) long. Its two main headstreams, the Black Volta and White Volta, begin in Burkina Faso. They join together in Ghana to form the Volta River, which then drains into the Gulf of Guinea.

In 1965, the Akosombo Dam was built along the Volta River south of Ajena. It holds back the Black and White Volta rivers. As a result, Lake Volta formed where the Black Volta and White Volta rivers meet. It is one of the largest artificial lakes in the world. Lake Bosumtwi in the Asante region of south-central Ghana is the country's only natural lake. It was formed when an asteroid struck about 1 million years ago. It is one of only a few **meteoritic** lakes on the planet.

Closer Look

Lake Volta and Akosombo Dam

Lake Volta accounts for nearly 4 percent of Ghana's area. The massive body of water spans 250 miles (400 km) long and covers 3,283 square miles (8,502 sq. km). About 15,000 homes and 740 villages were flooded when Lake Volta was first created. About 78,000 people had to move as a result of the flooding. But the lake brings many benefits to local people. It provides an affordable transportation link between communities in the coastal region and the northern savanna region.

Local farmers use water from Lake Volta as an affordable way to irrigate their crops. The lake also serves as a key fishing area. Akosombo Dam produces enough hydropower to supply most of Ghana's energy needs.

Akosombo Dam creates enough power to supply Ghana, with a surplus to sell to other countries.

Peak Places

The highest peak in Ghana, Mount Afadja, is just 2,887 feet (880 m) tall. It offers panoramic views of Togo, Lake Volta, and everything in between. Other peaks include Mount Edouka at 2,542 feet (775 m), Mount Atiwiredu at 2,539 feet (774 m), and Kwamisa Mountain at 2,479 feet (756 m). Most of Ghana's mountains are covered in tropical rain forests. They are found in the Volta Region, which is close to the Togo border.

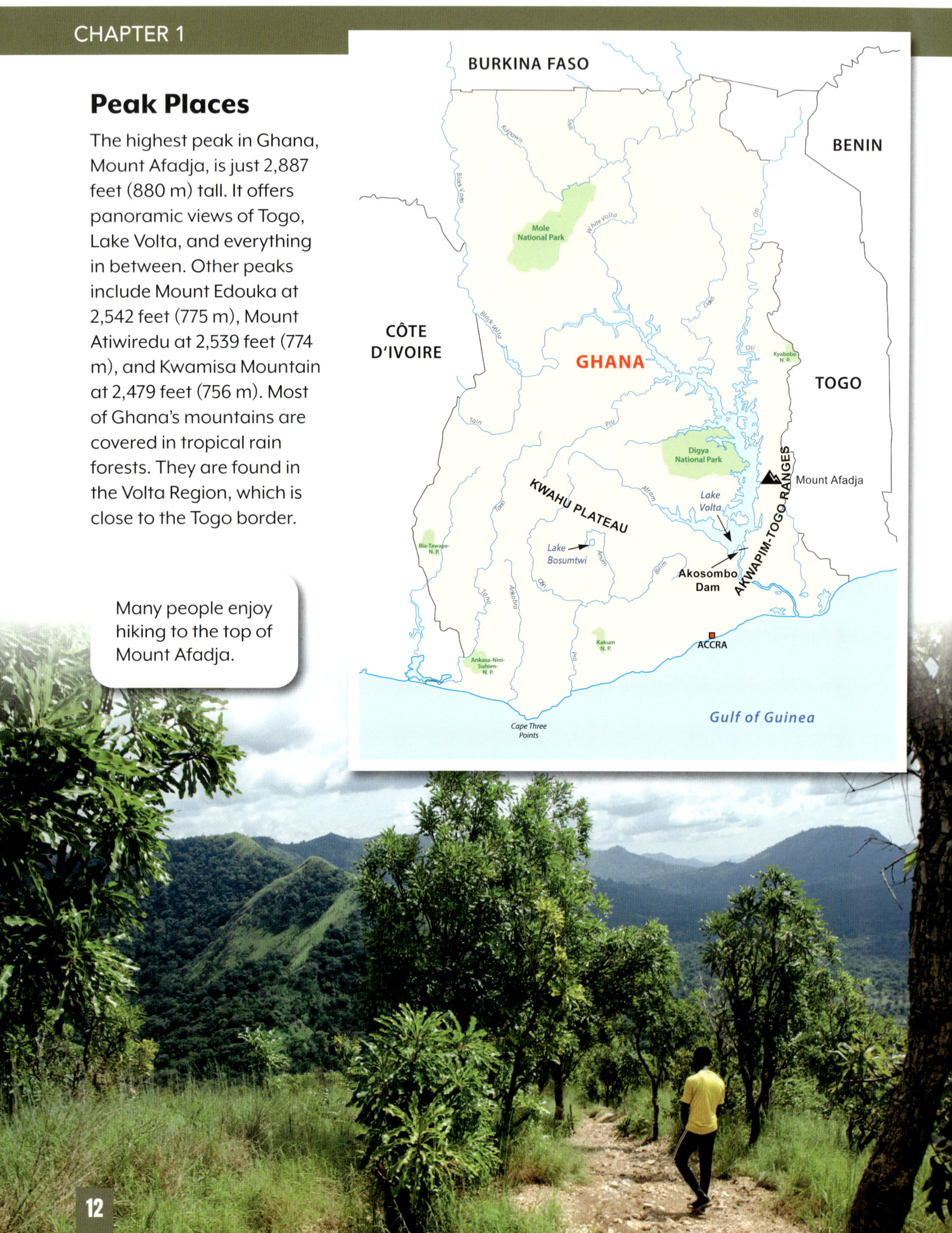

Many people enjoy hiking to the top of Mount Afadja.

African bush elephants are often seen at Mole National Park.

Animal Encounters

At one time, wildlife was plentiful across Ghana. But hunting and human development caused many animals to disappear or forced them off their lands. Seven national parks and several reserves have been set up across Ghana to help protect the country's wildlife. Many different animals make their homes in these places.

The colorful red-throated bee-eater is a common bird found throughout Ghana.

At Mole National Park near Damongo, elephants, hippopotamuses, and crocodiles can be spotted at watering holes. About 650 types of butterflies live in Kakum National Park near Cape Coast. Leopards, Diana monkeys, and scarlet-tailed African gray parrots are some of the other animals that live at this park. Manatees and otters can be found swimming in Ghana's lagoons. Hornbills, parrots, and vultures are a few of the bird species that live across the land, while the waters are filled with tuna, mackerel, herring, and other fish. There are also many smaller animals, such as snakes, lizards, and tortoises, that call Ghana home.

The western emperor swallowtail butterfly is one of the most common butterflies found in Kakum National Park.

Hot Topic

Ghana is known for its warm, tropical climate. Temperatures range from 70 to 90 degrees Fahrenheit (21 to 32 °C) throughout the year. Along the coast, cool winds blow in from the Atlantic Ocean and help ease the heat. While the southern part of the country is humid, the northern part is very dry. On average, the country gets about 47 inches (1,200 mm) of rainfall annually. The heaviest rains fall from April to July, and there are light rains from September through November each year.

People can tell the seasons in Ghana by looking at the vegetation. Dark green leaves mean it is the rainy season. Brown or leafless trees mean it is the dry season.

Closer Look

In some places, the extreme dryness of the air during harmattan season can cause trees to die.

When the dust in the air is heavy, as seen here in the Volta Region, it's known as the harmattan haze. It's similar to a heavy fog, but can last for days at a time.

Harmattan Winds

Between December and March, cool, dry winds wreak havoc across West Africa. They carry large amounts of dust from the Sahara and cause all kinds of problems, from traffic and flight delays to a greater risk of wildfires. A 2016 study found a connection between these harmattan winds and deadly **meningitis** outbreaks. Mucous membranes in the throat and lungs are damaged from the dust brought in from the harmattan winds, making people more susceptible to the disease. Visibility reduces to as little as 0.6 miles (1 km) when the dust blows in. Temperatures fall as low as 48 degrees Fahrenheit (9 °C). When combined with monsoons, tornadoes can form. Harmattan winds can spread dust hundreds of miles over the Atlantic Ocean.

CHAPTER 2

Kingdoms, Culture, and Colonialism

Ancient Ghana Empire

The Ghana Empire was the first trading empire of its kind in West Africa. It was very powerful and wealthy, and traded widely across the Sahara. It had a **monopoly** on West African gold and was known as the Land of the Gold.

The center of the empire was at least 500 miles (800 km) from the land now known as the Republic of Ghana. Historians are fairly certain that no part of the kingdom was located on any of the same lands that Ghana is today. Since the empire had no written language, all that is known about this powerful kingdom comes from the oral histories and medieval writings of Arabic traders who visited the area. While Ghanaians have many oral traditions that date back as far as the 14th century, they still came long after the disappearance of the Ghana Empire. As such, any connection between present-day Ghana and the ancient kingdom that shares its name remains unknown.

The Ghana Empire thrived between the 7th and 13th centuries and was located where Mali and Mauritania are currently found.

Kintampo Culture

The earliest evidence of humans in the Republic of Ghana dates back to about 50,000 B.C.E. Some people believe they came from the ancient Ghana Empire. Others think they came from the area now called the Republic of Benin or southwestern Nigeria. Archaeological findings show human settlements in present-day Ghana around 4,000 years ago. This early society was known as Kintampo. They made tools from wood, stone, and pottery. They also **domesticated** farm animals, cultivated the land, and mined valuable resources, such as metal and gold.

Pearl millet is a crop that grows well in hot climates. It is believed to be one of the first crops cultivated by the Kintampo people.

Some Kintampo buildings were built using panels of woven straw or reeds called wattle and covered with clay or animal dung known as daub.

Precolonial Ghana

By the late 13th century, much of Ghana was characterized by three zones that consisted of many smaller kingdoms or states. Each zone had its own political systems and ways of life. States in the northern zone were ruled by a supreme leader who had the power to make and enforce laws or declare war. Beneath the supreme leader were divisional chiefs and subchiefs who would rule over specific areas.

In the forest zone, families and individuals led centralized political units. The coastal zone had well-organized administrative and executive government branches that followed legal and **ethical** standards of society. A political council of chiefs and subchiefs ruled the coastal states. There was also a group of commoners who balanced the council's power by representing the voice of the people.

European Contact

In 1471, Portuguese mariners arrived on the coast of Ghana. They noticed the locals wearing gold jewelry and took great interest in the area. They began a trade relationship that initially benefited both the locals and the Portuguese. In exchange for gold, ivory, and pepper, local people received beads, metals, weapons, cloth, and liquor from the Portuguese. The area became known as the Gold Coast for its seemingly endless supply of gold.

For many years, the Portuguese had a monopoly on the gold trade with locals, but they knew it would not be long before other European countries wanted a piece of it. They began to **lease** lands along the coast from the local states and build fortresses, the first one being Elmina Castle in 1482. The forts were used for both defense and as a way to **facilitate** better trade relations with the locals. But the Portuguese could not maintain their hold, and by the 1600s, England, Denmark, Netherlands, **Prussia**, and Sweden had all started their own trade relationships in the area. By the late 1700s, Europeans had built more than 30 fortresses along the coast.

The Dutch took control of Elmina Castle from the Portuguese in 1637. Within the next five years, they forced the Portuguese out of the Gold Coast entirely.

European Impact

Permanent European settlements in the Gold Coast made trade relationships easier. It was much more convenient to send exports by sea to faraway places than via ancient overland trade routes to other parts of Africa. The forest zone, which had been the wealthiest in the country, began to decline as the coastal zone grew in wealth and power due to its European trade relationships.

Soon, traditional ways of life began to fade. Locals started to adopt more European ways of doing things. They began to eat differently as Europeans introduced new types of food, such as lemons, corn, bananas, and sugarcane. Locals learned to speak European languages and practice Christian beliefs. They also began to build stone houses similar to European homes.

The Portuguese built the first Christian church in Ghana just west of Elmina Castle. It was destroyed when the Dutch attacked in 1596. The Portuguese rebuilt the church inside the castle walls. It was altered after the Dutch took control, but the building still stands today.

The Slave Trade

Gold was not the only thing Europeans took from the area. Millions of people were enslaved and sent overseas. Most were sent to work in the Americas. As Europeans began to colonize the **New World**, they needed cheap labor to work on **plantations**. While many relied on **indentured servants** or the forced labor of **Indigenous** peoples, there was a larger demand than supply. People turned to West Africa to fulfill their needs. The slave trade was the most profitable business venture in the Gold Coast.

Fort Orange, located along the Gold Coast, was used to house enslaved people. When a ship arrived, enslaved individuals would be led out the "Door of No Return."

Within the Gold Coast, the slave trade was an established part of the country's culture long before Europeans arrived. While enslaved men and women were lower-class citizens with limited rights, they were often treated as members of their enslavers' families. By contrast, the slave trade in the Americas became a source of fear for locals because enslaved individuals were treated so poorly there. As more skilled workers were sent overseas, the Gold Coast started to experience its own labor shortage.

By the mid-1700s, some European nations began to condemn the slave trade. Over the next several decades, many countries stopped enslavement in West Africa. But demand for forced labor in the Americas continued. By 1807, it was illegal to import enslaved people into the United States, and Great Britain began measures to outlaw the slave trade on its own lands and around the world. However, other countries, such as Spain and Portugal, increased their interests in the slave trade to fill the void. It would take until the 1860s to finally stop the practice.

Monuments, such as this one in the Volta Region, are reminders of the hardships and suffering the Ghanaians faced during the slave trade.

Enslavement in Ghana

Over time, the slave trade created more wealth than the gold trade in Ghana. Though the exact number is unknown, historians estimate that about 5,000 enslaved individuals were shipped from Ghana to the Americas each year between the 16th and 17th centuries. There were many ways a person could become enslaved. Some were purchased or offered as a way to repay a debt. Others were enslaved after being taken as prisoners of war or as a form of punishment for criminal acts. Wars were fought solely as a means to capture and enslave locals.

Before it was used to house enslaved people, the Cape Coast Castle was used to trade timber and gold.

When the slave trade became profitable, large underground dungeons were added to Cape Coast Castle to hold enslaved people waiting for export.

Enslaved people were packed so tightly on ships that they didn't even have room to turn around. Ships could hold anywhere from 250–600 enslaved individuals.

Colonial Rule

For years, European nations battled for control of the Gold Coast. Eventually, Great Britain became the dominant European nation. In 1874, the Gold Coast officially became a British colony. With it came a period of colonial rule through which Great Britain controlled the area. The powerful Asante empire attempted to fight back but was defeated. Great Britain absorbed the Asante along with the many other kingdoms and states in the area.

The Asante and the British were involved in five different wars between 1823 and 1900, known as the Anglo-Ashanti (Asante) Wars. The last one ended with the Asante becoming part of the British colony.

Closer Look

Asante Empire

The Asante empire was a mighty southern state that spread from the Comoé River to the Togo Mountains in the 1700s and 1800s. The Asante played a key role in the slave trade by supplying British and Dutch traders with enslaved men and women. In return, the Asante received weapons, which they used to defend and grow their territory. When the British outlawed the export of enslaved people, it caused tension with the Asante. Over the next several decades, the Asante challenged the British many times over various issues. On January 1, 1902, the empire became a British colony.

Achieving Independence

British colonialism was a time of great economic advancement in the Gold Coast. It also led to the unification of different kingdoms and states under one country. But it brought violence, harm, and inequality for Ghanaians. Locals began to demand independence for their country. In the years after World War II, these cries for freedom from British rule grew louder.

In 1949, political activist Kwame Nkrumah formed a party called the Convention People's Party (CPP). He coordinated strikes, boycotts, protests, and other acts of **noncooperation** with the colonial government. Nkrumah was eventually elected to Parliament and on March 22, 1952, was sworn in as the Gold Coast's first prime minister. Nkrumah continued his campaign for self-government, and on March 6, 1957, he announced the country had gained independence from British colonial rule. It was the first sub-Saharan African nation to achieve this status.

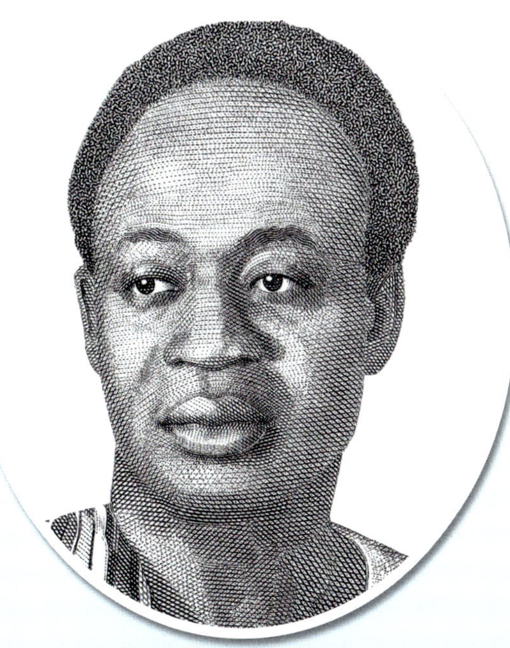

Kwame Nkrumah (1909–1972)

During his campaign of **nonviolent activism**, Nkrumah was arrested for his part and spent one year in prison. It was during this time that he was elected to Parliament, winning a majority of votes in Ghana's first general elections.

A New Ghana

The new nation was named Ghana in honor of the once-thriving African empire. It was a major milestone for the entire African continent and people of African descent across the globe. However, in the decades that followed, Ghana would face much political instability. It experienced everything from **coups**, corruption, and mismanagement on its path to becoming the successful **democratic** country it is today.

Fall from Power

Nkrumah vowed to continue his fight against colonialism and help secure independence for other African nations. Under his leadership, Ghana ushered in many economic and **infrastructure** development projects. New roads and health care facilities were built. The Bank of Ghana and Black Star Line shipping were created, and the Volta River Project began. On July 1, 1960, Ghana became a republic within the **British Commonwealth**. This brought a new constitution and greater levels of power and control to Nkrumah, the republic's newly elected president.

Over time, Nkrumah became a more **authoritarian** leader. People began to resent the policies and practices he put in place. The economy began to crumble and much of the government work fell into the hands of dishonest politicians. People began to protest for change. On February 24, 1966, Nkrumah was overthrown in a coup led by Ghanaian military and police forces.

The Black Star Gate stands in the center of Independence Square, also known as Black Star Square. It is one of three monuments built in the square to commemorate the independence of Ghana.

Moving Forward

Over the next several decades, Ghanaians experienced a range of leaders and leadership styles. Many circumstances caused their economy to rise and fall. Today, Ghana is headed by Nana Addo Dankwa Akufo-Addo. Akufo-Addo promised Ghanaians he would revive the economy, and he quickly went to work on making it happen. He put a program into place that would see the development of at least one factory in each key district. The economy started to grow, but the COVID-19 pandemic slowed it down. Key exports, such as cocoa and oil, sold for lower than average to other parts of the world. The tourism and service sectors were the most affected during the pandemic. Sales in the hotel and restaurant industries were down almost 40 percent in 2020. The government has put some initiatives in place to assist households and businesses with acquired losses, and hopefully help revive the economy.

Akufo-Addo was sworn in for his second term as president of Ghana in January 2021.

Cocoa beans were brought to the Gold Coast in the 1870s. Since then, they have become Ghana's main cash crop, making Ghana the second-largest cocoa producer in the world.

CHAPTER 3

Ghana Today

Developing Nation

Ghana's economy is growing. Thanks to the discovery of oil reserves in 2007, it is now a lower-middle-income country and much has been done to decrease poverty levels. However, most Ghanaians still work in low-paying agricultural jobs, and there is a large gap between the poorest and wealthiest people. Housing, employment, health care, and sanitation remain a problem in much of the country.

In recent years, large numbers of people have moved from rural areas to urban centers in search of work in factories and offices.

Closer Look

Water Collection

In many rural villages, women or young girls get up early to collect water. Many people rely on nearby lakes and rivers for their water supply. These sources of water are often **contaminated** and unclean. For many people, a trip to get water can take at least 30 minutes, walking barefoot or in rubber flip-flops. The trip home is even more difficult as they carry their full containers on their heads. This can have long-term health effects for their heads, necks, and shoulders, as many have to make this trip several times a day. While many in urban areas now have access to clean water, there are still 4.4 million people in Ghana who do not.

About 70 percent of people in Accra rely on tro-tros, an informal system of mini-buses that run throughout the city. They are low-cost, and routes change based on riders' needs.

Village Life

Traditionally, most Ghanaians live in villages as farmers. The roads in these villages are often unpaved and in poor condition. The homes are built from materials that are easily found in the area. In most places, clay and straw are used to make bricks for the walls. The roof can be made from clay or thatched palm leaves and grass. Inside, Borassus palm is used for the beams because it resists insects. There are an average of 10 to 12 rooms in a house, with no running water or electricity. Most have poor **ventilation** and no bathroom. Women cook outdoors and people often dine together in the courtyard.

Ghana's Cities

Accra is the nation's capital and one of its most **populous** cities. While there is much poverty in Accra, the city is evolving. It is always improving its infrastructure and becoming more like other major cities around the world. In urban areas, roads are paved and well maintained, and there is a public transportation system that makes it easier for people to get from one part of the city to another. However, because of rapid urbanization there is a severe housing shortage. Millions of housing units are needed to keep up with the demand. These low-income compound houses consist of 8 to 15 single-story units built around a central courtyard, often with a shared kitchen and bathroom. With rising mortgage and land prices, many find it hard to afford even these low-cost homes.

Increased Health Care

Ghana has a government-run health program called the National Health Insurance Scheme (NHIS). It provides affordable health insurance for people of all income levels. Since the NHIS was put in place, death rates have lowered across Ghana, and there are better treatments for people with illnesses or diseases. There are also medical facilities operated by religious organizations. Most health care facilities are located in major cities and towns. While they provide decent care, they are not up to Western standards. Access to health care is not as readily available in rural villages, and doctor availability in these places is limited.

Many people in rural areas do not have the means to travel to hospitals. They rely on nurses and pharmacies that focus on care for high-risk diseases, such as **malaria**. Traditional African medicine is still common in parts of Ghana as well. Practitioners use herbal cures, medicinal plants, prayer, and other tactics to help people in need.

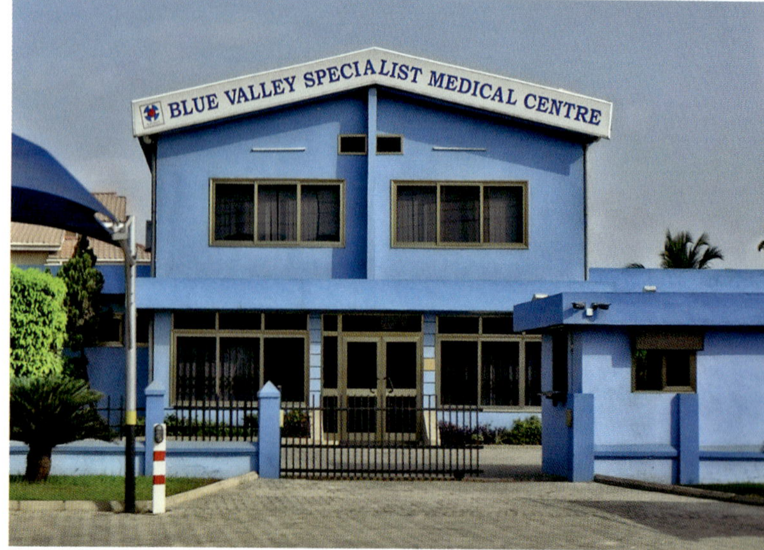

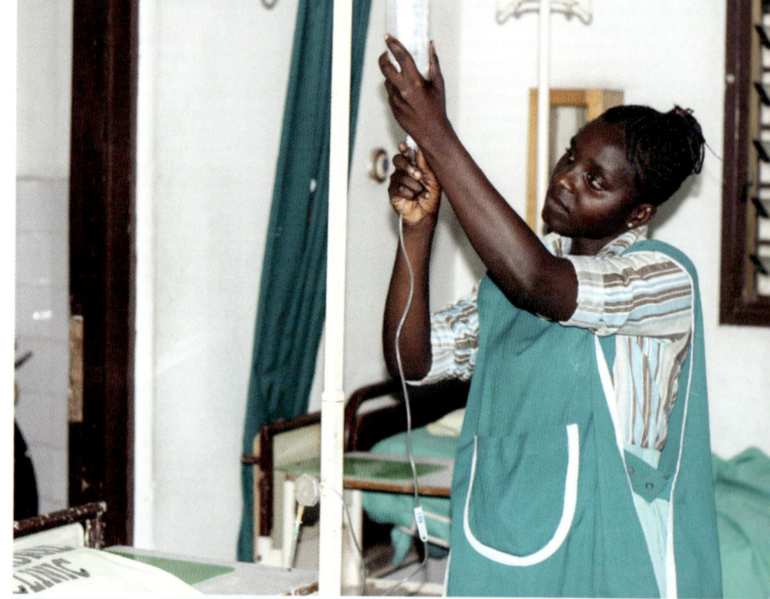

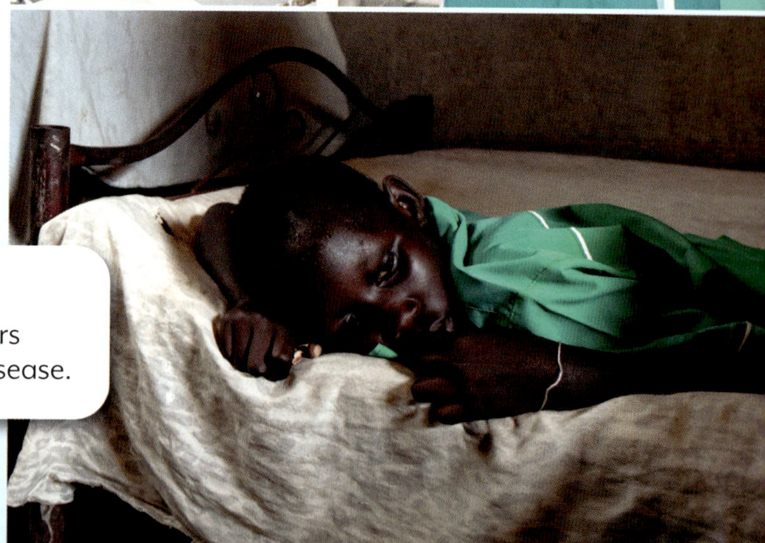

Malaria is a leading cause of death in Ghana. Children and expectant mothers have a higher risk of contracting the disease.

There are about 140 institutions in Ghana that offer postsecondary education. Only a small number of Ghanaians attend university, college, or other postsecondary schools. Graduates often have higher-paying jobs and better quality of life as a result.

Eye on Education

Despite the country's many hardships, education is a priority in Ghana. The local education system is one of the best in West Africa and many other sub-Saharan countries. Most children have access to two years of kindergarten and six years of primary education. They can also attend three years of junior secondary schooling and three years of senior secondary schooling. In 2017, Ghana made secondary schooling free for everyone, so enrollment climbed from 57 percent in 2012 to 73 percent in 2017.

Access to education is more limited in rural areas. In these places, there are low enrollment rates in schools. Children that do attend schools often have to walk long distances to spend only a few hours in broken-down huts with limited teaching materials. In cities and towns, there are more teachers and better facilities. Children attend schools in concrete buildings that have desks, chairs, and other resources.

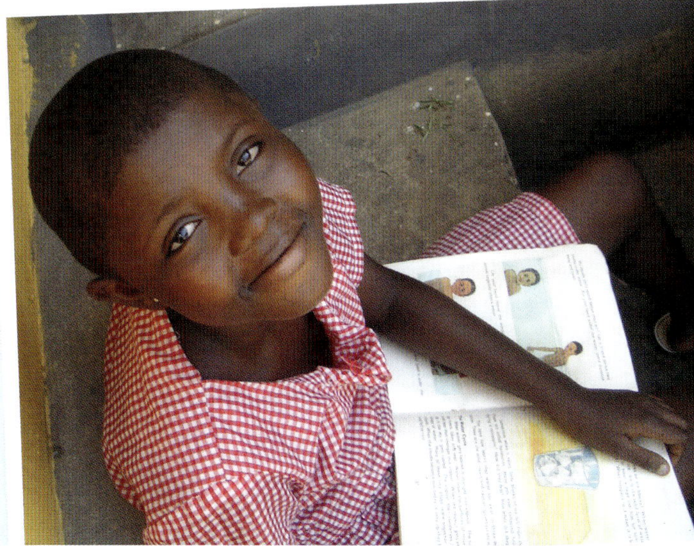

About 80 percent of Ghanaians are literate.

Getting Around

Ghana is making headway in the area of transportation, but it has a long way to go. Privately owned vehicles are the preferred way of getting around in Accra. Buses run between larger cities and towns, but travel to more rural areas is still a challenge. Ghana has three airlines and 10 airports. Of them, three have paved runways, and most only provide service to domestic airlines. Along with Kotoka International Airport in Accra, the airports in Tamale and Kumasi receive passengers from all over the world.

Important Industries

Ghana's economy is mainly dependent on the export of gold, cocoa, oil, and gas. The economy rises and falls with the prices of these products. About 45 percent of Ghana's workforce is employed in the agriculture sector, which accounts for about 21 percent of the nation's wealth. Industries such as mining, timber, aluminum smelting, food processing, cement, and small commercial shipbuilding contribute about 32 percent of the nation's wealth. Most Ghanaians export their farm products, but they also grow crops for use at home and to sell at local markets. Fishing is an important industry. Offshore trawlers harvest fish for both domestic and overseas markets.

Railroads, which are mainly used to transport freight, provide service within the "golden triangle," which includes the major southern cities of Sekondi-Takoradi, Kumasi, and Accra.

Traditional Indigenous canoes are used to fish inshore and supply local communities and markets.

Cocoa beans are covered by a white pulp inside a hard pod, or shell.

Cocoa Production

Africa produces about 3.5 million tons (3.2 million metric tons) of cocoa beans each year. Ghana and Côte d'Ivoire are the largest producers. Droughts due to **climate change**, lack of knowledge about farming, disease, and pests pose challenges to cocoa production. The Ghana Cocoa Board, or Cocobod, governs cocoa research, production, and marketing across the country, while the Cocoa Research Institute of Ghana oversees manufacturing and farming practices. They have put programs in place to help educate farmers about better farming techniques and how to improve crops through the use of fertilizers, drought-resistant seedlings, hand pollination methods, and the installation of wells for irrigation.

In 2021, Ghana had its largest cocoa harvest ever, but the COVID-19 pandemic resulted in less demand and lower prices for the beans. Currently, most of Ghana's cocoa wealth comes from exporting the beans to other parts of the world. Globally, the retail chocolate industry is valued at more than $100 billion U.S. ($131 billion CDN), but Ghana earns just $2 billion U.S. ($2.6 billion CDN). This is because Ghana processes and manufactures only about 30 to 40 percent of its cocoa bean harvest into chocolate and semi-finished products, such as liquor and cocoa butter. President Akufo-Addo is working to improve this number.

CHAPTER 4

Cultural Diversity

Ghana is a new country, and there is no written record of its history prior to contact with Europeans. It was created by bringing together many Indigenous societies, each with their own culture and traditions that carry on today. Despite their diverse backgrounds, the people of Ghana have a strong sense of national unity and are advocates for **pan-Africanism**. However, the country is still developing its unique national identity, which continues to evolve and grow.

Ghana has a young population. Nearly 60 percent of people are under the age of 25.

Diverse Society

Most people in Ghana are of Black African descent. The country is home to many different ethnicities. Akan is the largest, making up nearly half of Ghana's population. It includes the Anyi, Asante, Baule, Fante, and Guang peoples. Other large groups include the Mole-Dagbani, Ewe, and Ga-Dangme, which together account for another 40 percent of the nation's population. Each group has its own unique culture and heritage. There have been some conflicts between Ghana's ethnic groups throughout history, but most groups live peacefully together and embrace their varied customs, traditions, and beliefs.

The Larabanga Mosque in the northern region is the oldest mosque in Ghana. It is the place of worship for many Muslims.

Talk to Me

There are as many as 75 different languages spoken among Ghana's different ethnic groups. Most Ghanaians speak one of these as their first language. However, many speak multiple languages. In an effort to help unify the country, English is the official language. It is the language of business, and it is mandatory for children to use it in school. There are nine other government-sponsored languages in addition to English.

Customs and Beliefs

Christianity was introduced to locals when Europeans arrived, and today it is the most widespread religion across Ghana. Many people are religious and attend church weekly. Easter and Christmas are the most important Christian holidays in Ghana. About 20 percent of the population is Muslim, and most live in the northern part of the country. There are also a small number of people who follow ancestral Indigenous belief systems. Traditional religions have some common traits. They all believe there is a supreme being and that the natural world and the spirit world are connected. There is also a great respect for chiefs, elders, and priests, as well as deceased ancestors.

English is the language found on billboards in cities such as Accra.

One ritual during the Homowo Festival is to sprinkle *Kpokpoi* in front of heritage sites and people's homes.

Celebrations

Ghana is a vibrant country that comes alive through many annual festivals and **rites** ceremonies that are held in honor of major milestones, such as marriage and birth. The Odwira Festival is celebrated by the people of Akropong-Akuapem, Aburi, Larteh, and Mamfi in September and October each year. It is a time of spiritual cleansing when people pray for protection and thank their ancestors for the harvest.

Homowo is one of the largest festivals in Ghana. Its name means "to hoot at hunger." It was first celebrated by the Ga people to mark the end of a long drought and **famine**. Homowo takes place in May each year. There is singing and dancing, and people eat a dish called *Kpokpoi*, which is made from palm oil and cornmeal.

When a person dies, their life is celebrated in an elaborate funeral. Some Ghanaians believe the souls of the dead are reunited with their ancestors, and then they are reborn into the same family line. Babies might be named after deceased family members and are even sometimes referred to as mother, father, uncle, and so on. The hope is that the baby will take on all the good qualities of that person.

Smaller families are becoming more common, especially in urban centers, and gender roles are less specific than they once were.

Family Matters

Traditionally, elders would arrange marriages. The groom's family would pay a price to the bride's family. Sometimes, men would have more than one wife. This was a sign of their status, and chiefs would often take many wives. It meant they had enough wealth to pay for multiple brides and provide for several families. Today, **polygamy** is less common, and people often choose their own partners. Most stay within their own ethnic group.

Family plays a central role for most Ghanaians. Many generations often live together in the same household, especially in rural areas. In some cases, husbands and wives continue to live with their individual families after they wed. In other cases, they might both move in with either the husband's or wife's family. Where they live depends on the customs of their ethnic group. In all cases, men are the heads of the household and women take care of the home and children. Teens help out around the house and care for their brothers and sisters when they are not in school or studying.

The Akan people often perform a dance called *Adowa* at festivals, funerals, and celebrations.

Respect for Others

Ghanaians are expected to treat others with respect, especially elders or anyone older than themselves. They take great care when greeting each other, and it is very disrespectful not to greet an elder first and offer to help them in any way they might need. Formal titles are always used when possible. Otherwise, informal titles, such as sir, madam, auntie, uncle, father, or grandma, are acceptable. All sentences start with "please" when speaking to an elder.

Ghanaians are typically polite and quiet around others. This is especially true for women. People are careful not to share too much information about themselves. Public shows of affection are not acceptable. People of the same age and gender may hold hands as a sign of friendship. Any other public displays of affection for men and women are not acceptable in public places, even if they are married.

Cultural Cuisine

Ghana is known for its hot and spicy traditional foods. Key ingredients include yams, cassava, maize, beans, and plantains. Rice is a staple, and it is often served with sauce. Palm nut, groundnut, and millet soups are also common. They usually contain peppers and other vegetables, and a protein, such as fish. Many families raise chickens or goats to eat on special occasions.

Colorful Cloth

Traditional clothing is still common in rural areas and is mostly worn for festivals and special events. Each ethnic group in Ghana has its own unique form of traditional dress. Wooden looms are used to weave cotton, raffia, and wool into the Gonja cloth of the northern people, and Kente cloth of the Ewe and Asante peoples.

In Ghanaian culture, the left hand is considered dirty and should never be offered in greeting.

Fufu is one of the most popular dishes in Ghana. It is made by mashing boiled cassava and plantain together and shaping the mixture into balls with a small indentation. *Fufu* is used like a spoon to scoop up soup or stew and then swallowed. No chewing required!

Closer Look

Kente Cloth

Kente is the best-known Ghanaian fabric, and one of the most recognizable African textiles. It dates back to the Asante empire more than 400 years ago, but might be even older than that. At first, only the ruler could wear Kente, but over time, others in positions of power or importance were also permitted to wear it. The cloth became a status symbol.

Men wear Kente like a dress and drape it across one shoulder. Women wear it as part of a two-piece outfit that includes a skirt and shawl. The bright colors and more than 300 unique patterns of Kente cloth have special meanings. For instance, gold represents wealth, green symbolizes plants, and blue stands for the sky.

Kente is made with a mixture of black, red, blue, gold or yellow, green, white, and purple cloth.

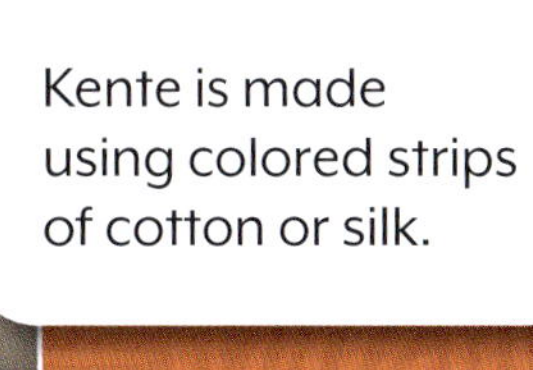

Kente is made using colored strips of cotton or silk.

Arts and Entertainment

Indigenous music, drumming, and dance are important to the culture and heritage of Ghana. The Institute for African Studies at the University of Ghana provides training for the performing arts and hosts many events each year that showcase traditional dancers and musicians. Highlife is a contemporary style of dance music that began to gain popularity in Ghana in the 1930s. It blends together traditional Indigenous music and European influences, such as brass bands.

This traditional Asante mask is made from metal and wood.

Creative Crafts

Wood carving, pottery making, metal sculpting, goldsmithing, and weaving are some of the traditional art forms that Ghanaians are known for. Historically, crafts were made mainly for practical or ceremonial purposes. Everything had a use, such as wooden stools and game boards, metal swords, and clay dishware. Today, there is a rising arts scene in Ghana, and pieces are often created for enjoyment or pleasure.

Basket weaving is a traditional skill many women learn.

Golden Stool

The Asante made ornate ceremonial stools for chiefs and other important leaders. They were carved from wood and covered in gold leaf. The tradition dates back to the 1600s, when legend says a Golden Stool that houses the souls of the Asante people came down from the heavens. No one ever sat on the stool, and it never touched the ground. New kings were raised and lowered over the sacred Golden Stool, but they would not touch it. Chiefs consulted at the stool before going into war, and they won many victories. Today, the Golden Stool remains a powerful symbol of the Asante empire, and it is still part of ceremonies crowning traditional rulers.

The final war of the Anglo-Ashanti Wars began because a British representative wanted to sit on the Golden Stool.

Culture and Heritage

There are numerous cultural institutions and **UNESCO World Heritage sites** throughout Ghana that showcase the nation's rich cultural heritage. Elmina Castle, Kakum National Park, Christiansborg Castle, Kwame Nkrumah Memorial Park, Du Bois Centre, and Cape Coast are a few examples.

Ghana is also home to many monuments that reflect the history of colonialism and the slave trade in Africa. There are about 80 castles and colonial buildings along a 300-mile (483 km) stretch of Ghana's Atlantic coast. They represent nearly 70 percent of all colonial structures on the West African shoreline, and they give people a unique glimpse into what it was like to be imprisoned and enslaved in Africa.

The seat of government of Ghana had been at Christiansborg Castle since 1902. It recently moved to Golden Jubilee House, since many argued that the government should not be in a building where enslaved people were once kept.

CHAPTER 5

Growth and National Unity

As a result of the slave trade, many Ghanaians are part of the African **diaspora**. There are an estimated 200 million Africans spread all over the world who have a limited connection to their homelands, millions of them being of Ghanaian descent. The UN General Assembly launched the International Decade for People of African Descent from 2015 to 2024. The goal is to support the recognition, justice, and development of Africans who have been victims of **systemic racism** and exclusion throughout history, and help strengthen the connection between the diaspora and Africa. President Akufo-Addo of Ghana announced the Year of Return in 2019 as a way to encourage the African diaspora to return to their homelands and commemorate the 400-year anniversary of the arrival of the first enslaved Africans in the Americas. Ghana launched many programs and initiatives to help people reconnect with their roots and **repatriate** them into the country. These programs included everything from help with buying a home to setting up bank accounts and finding work.

It is believed the Year of Return brought about 250,000 extra visitors to Ghana in 2019.

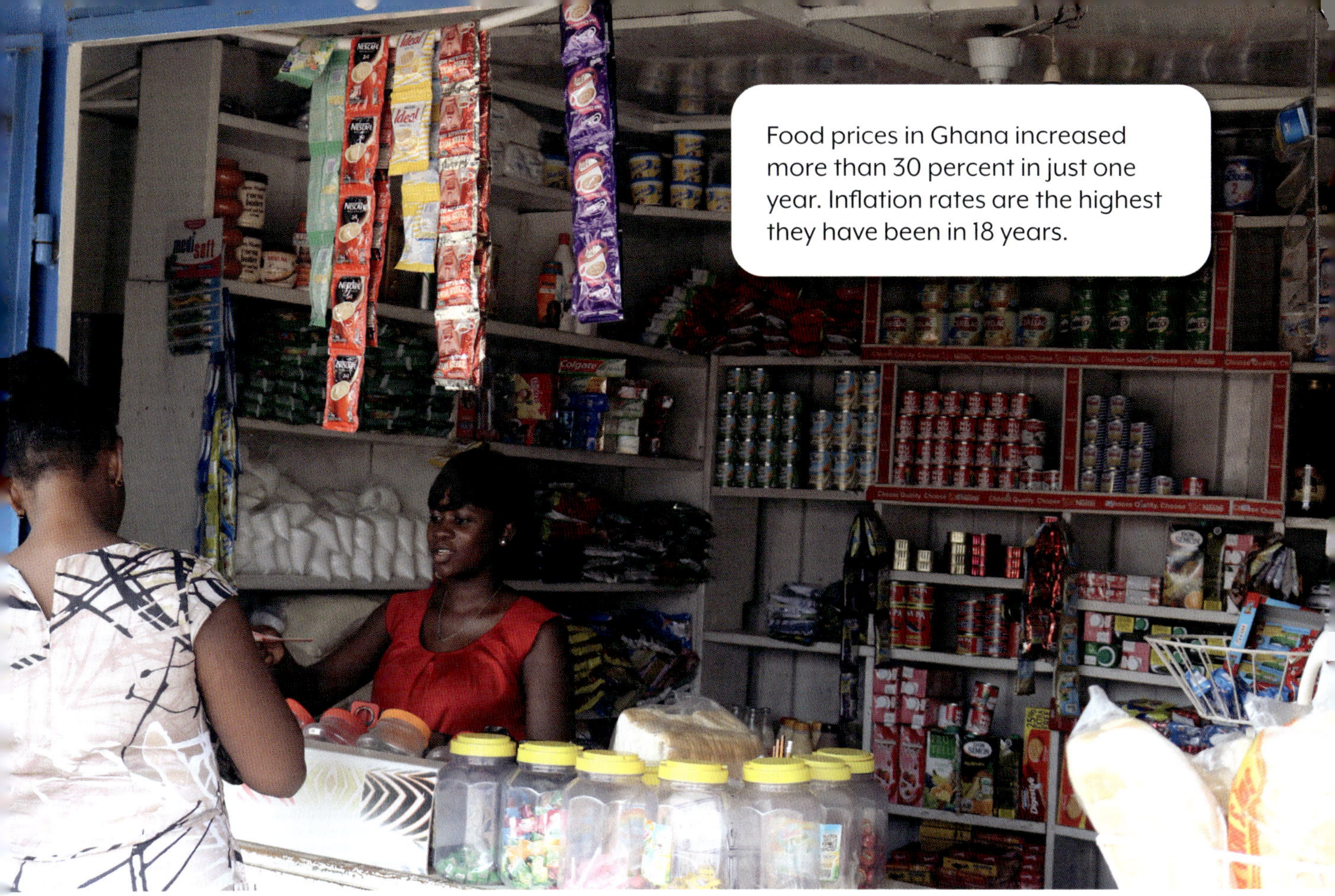

Food prices in Ghana increased more than 30 percent in just one year. Inflation rates are the highest they have been in 18 years.

Economic Growth

Ghana experienced about 7 percent economic growth in 2019, placing it among the top 10 fast-growing economies in Africa. The nation's wealth is largely due to its vast natural resources, large-scale cocoa production, and the discovery of oil reserves in the 2000s. However, Ghana's rapid rise came to a crashing stop during the COVID-19 pandemic, with its economic growth falling as low as 0.4 percent. As a result, the poverty rate and national debt increased, putting the country at risk.

However, the economy took a sharp turn in the right direction in 2021, with 4.1 percent growth. That number is expected to continue to climb, which will help Ghana recover to pre-pandemic levels. Still, **inflation** rates across the country remain high, and have been further compounded by the war in Ukraine that started in February 2022. This has caused a global increase in the price of food, fertilizers, fuels, and metals needed for manufacturing.

Countrywide Challenges

Across Ghana, there are inequalities between urban centers and rural communities that lack infrastructure and resources. Many communities do not have adequate roads that allow for smooth travel to cities where they can access services and sell their wares.

Malnutrition due to food insecurity is a problem for many Ghanaians, especially those living in the north where there is only one rainy season for growing. Farmers face challenges due to decreasing prices, workers moving to urban areas, poor roads, and unsustainable farming practices.

Climate change has resulted in unpredictable and extreme weather patterns and rising sea levels. Warmer temperatures and less rain, as well as droughts, forest fires, coastal erosion, and flash floods are all becoming more common. In 2020, the government of Ghana established the National Adaptation Plan (NAP) to reduce the negative impacts of climate change over the next several decades. In addition, the government is taking measures to reduce resource depletion caused by small-scale mining and forestry operations that do not have land **reclamation** and **reforestation** plans.

This fishing village in Ghana has been flooded due to a flash flood.

Fighting Poverty

Ghana quickly began to reduce its poverty levels by 2 percent per year after it returned to democracy in the early 1990s. But by 1998, those results began to slow yearly, dipping as low as 0.2 percent between 2012 and 2016. Despite strong economic growth, income is distributed very unevenly among Ghanaians and the country has high overall poverty rates. The gap between the richest 10 percent of people and the poorest 10 percent continues to grow, with the top 10 percent of income earners consuming 6.8 times more than the lowest income earners in 2016.

Unlike the poor who live in small, cramped homes, often with unsafe conditions, the wealthy live in large, beautiful homes in Ghana's prime locations.

Closer Look

Multidimensional Poverty

Multidimensional poverty means not only a lack of money, but also includes other factors, such as poor health, lack of education, and inadequate housing. It affects about 65 percent of people in rural communities and only 27 percent of those living in urban areas. With the help of the United Nations Development Programme (UNDP), as well as other organizations such as The Hunger Project, the Ghanaian government is working to reduce poverty and improve conditions for everyone. Ghana now serves as a role model to other African nations seeking to eliminate poverty.

The Hunger Project helps Ghanaians gain knowledge of the technologies available to them.

Solar-powered irrigation pumps are one way the UNDP is helping maximize crop yields in rural villages.

Looking Forward

Learning about the physical geography of Ghana involves getting to know its borders as a nation and the cities and towns within those borders. However, it is also about studying human conditions within the country throughout time. It involves learning about how Ghanaians have adjusted their ways of life, cultural beliefs, and traditions to reflect the landscape, natural resources, climate, and other physical features of the land. Geography and the environment shaped the lives of Ghanaians in the past and will continue to do so into the future.

Finding out how Ghanaians have impacted the physical geography of their country and how that can alter the landscape and conditions is also important. Learning about both past and present conditions can help the people of Ghana plan for the future. Throughout history, there has been evidence of how Ghanaians have adapted their ways of life around their physical geography and how the physical geography has also changed as a result of their activities.

By understanding their relationship with the land, Ghanaians can make informed decisions that continuously improve their lives. More and more young people are hopeful about the future and believe that hard work and education will help make it brighter.

Installing wells is a way Ghanaians can get clean, safe water in the dry areas of their country.

Ghanaians are hard workers. With a little help, innovation, and leadership, Ghanaians can find better ways to work within their environment to reduce poverty and hunger.

assets Things that belong to a person

authoritarian Relating to a strict form of government where the leader is not answerable to the people

British Commonwealth An association of nations including the United Kingdom and former British colonies

cacao A South American tree containing cocoa seeds used to make chocolate

climate change The long-term changes in the average conditions of the world's temperature and weather patterns

colonial Relating to a colony, or a country or area occupied by and under the control of another country

contaminated Something that is harmful or polluted

coup Violent overthrow of a government

cultivation The act of preparing and using soil for growing plants or crops

deciduous A type of tree that sheds its leaves in autumn

democratic A form of government in which people choose leaders by voting

diaspora A large group of people who settled away from their home country or traditional homeland

domesticate To tame animals to keep as pets or livestock

economic The study of the economy, or the part of society that creates wealth

ethical Relating to morals, or what is right and wrong

facilitate To make something easier

famine A situation where a large number of people do not have enough food to eat

Greenwich meridian An imaginary line at 0° longitude, also known as the prime meridian

indentured servants A laborer contracted to work for another person for a specific amount of time, in exchange for accommodation, food, or other goods

Indigenous Native to a particular place. Indigenous peoples are the original inhabitants of a place.

inflation An increase in prices of goods and services

infrastructure The equipment or structures, such as roads and water supply, that a country or region needs to function properly

lease To use something for a period of time in return for payment

malaria A serious disease that causes symptoms such as fever and that is passed from one person to another through the bite of a mosquito

meningitis A disease that causes swelling in the brain and spine

meteoritic Referring to or caused by rocks that have fallen from space

monopoly A situation where there is a single seller or supplier of a product or service

natural resources Materials or substances that occur in nature that can be used or sold

New World Referring to the western hemisphere, specifically North and South America

noncooperation Refusing to cooperate, often as a form of protest

nonviolent activism A way of protesting or campaigning for change without physical violence or force

pan-Africanism The idea that all peoples of African descent have common interests and should be unified

plantations Large farms used to grow crops such as tobacco, sugar, or coffee

polygamy The practice of being married to more than one person at a time

populous Having a large population

Prussia A former German state in Europe along the southeast coast of the Baltic Sea

reclamation The act of reclaiming or restoring something to its original state, or something new and better

reforestation The act of replanting trees in an area where there used to be a forest

repatriate To send someone back to their homeland

republic A state in which power is held by the people and elected representatives

rites Religious rituals, customs, or ceremonies

smallholder farms Small farms, often under 5 acres (2 hectares) in size and used for subsistence farming of a single family

sub-Saharan The area of Africa that lies south of the Sahara

subsistence The state of having just enough to survive

systemic racism Forms of racism that are embedded in laws or written policies

UNESCO World Heritage site A protected landmark or area singled out by the United Nations Educational, Scientific, and Cultural Organization as being globally significant

ventilation The process of bringing fresh air into a room or building

Books

Blauer, Ettagale, and Jason Laure. *Ghana.* Children's Press, 2009.

Smith, Elliott. *The Slave Trade: Black Lives and the Drive for Profit.* Lerner Publications, 2022.

Soper, Dorothy Brown. *We Are Akan: Our People and Our Kingdom in the Rainforest, Ghana, 1807.* Luminare Press, 2021.

Websites

Learn more about Ghana's history, land, and people:
www.britannica.com/place/Ghana

Stay current on the latest news about Ghana:
https://news.un.org/en/tags/ghana

Find out more facts about Ghana:
www.cia.gov/the-world-factbook/countries/ghana/#introduction

About the Author

Heather C. Hudak has written hundreds of kids' books on all kinds of topics. She loves to travel when she's not writing. Heather has visited about 60 countries and hopes to travel to Ghana one day.